THE AMERICAN IMAGE

THE AMERICAN IMAGE

Photographs from the National Archives, 1860-1960

With an introduction by Alan Trachtenberg

Exhibitions staff
Office of Educational Programs
National Archives and Records Service
General Services Administration
Washington, D.C.

Pantheon Books
New York

Library of Congress Cataloging in Publication Data
National Archives Trust Fund Board.
The American image.
1. United States—Description and travel—
Views—Catalogs. 2. United States—History—
1865–   —Pictorial works—Catalogs.
3. United States. National Archives—Photograph
collections—Catalogs.   I. Title.
E168.N28 1979   016.973′022′2   79-1878
ISBN 0-394-50798-3
ISBN 0-394-73815-2 pbk.

Manufactured in the United States of America
468975
Designed by Robert Aulicino

Contents

This book is based on an exhibition, *The American Image:* Photographs from the Archives of the United States, 1860–1960, which opened in the Circular Gallery of the National Archives Building in November 1979. The book was compiled by Christina Rudy, Exhibitions staff, under the direction of Caryl Marsh, Curator of Exhibitions and Research.

NOTE ON THE PHOTOGRAPHS

When selecting the photographs for this book from the 5 million in our holdings, it became necessary to impose some arbitrary limits on our search. Thus, we decided to concentrate on pictures taken in the United States and thereby omitted large numbers of fine photographs taken in other countries. Also, we selected none of the relatively few color photographs in the Archives. The scope of our holdings also affects our coverage of several topics. For instance, we have full United States Navy and Coast Guard coverage of World War II, but only a few photographs after 1938 from the Army, Air Force, and Marine Corps.

Finally, the caption information set off in quotation marks is taken directly from the original written materials accompanying the photographs. If the original records were incomplete, we sometimes included additional information if it was available.

Foreword

In 1978, more than 3000 people—historians, political scientists, economists, photographers, Civil War buffs—researched the 5 million photographs in the holdings of the National Archives in Washington, D.C. The purpose of this book and the exhibition on which it is based is to make these holdings known to an even wider audience. We hope the book will also serve as an invitation for research to scholars unfamiliar with the holdings of our Still Picture Branch.

To select the photographs for this book from more than 5 million was a formidable task. Our original criteria were that each photograph be both visually arresting and historically interesting. A team composed of archivists familiar with the holdings, exhibit specialists, and knowledgeable volunteers made a preliminary selection of more than 1000 photographs. From this initial pool, the next selection was made by a jury that included Albert Meisel, Assistant Archivist for Educational Programs; William H. Leary, Archivist, Still Picture Branch; Will Stapp, Curator of Photography, National Portrait Gallery; and Samuel Wagstaff, Jr., a photo historian and scholar. These four narrowed the choices down to about 400 photos. Discussion by the staff of the Still Picture Branch and exhibit specialists narrowed the field even further until the jury of four and the exhibit specialists decided on the final 250 photographs, from which the publisher selected the ones you see in this book.

We realize that each individual selection cannot satisfy everyone, but we believe that the varied knowledge, background, and tastes of those who selected the photographs have resulted in a rich, vibrant view of American people and places from 1860 to 1960. There is something here to delight, amaze, and inform each of us.

Each of these photographs comes from collections compiled by government agencies and judged to be permanently valuable as an official record. Wherever possible, the caption information is taken from the documentation accompanying the photograph and has been quoted directly. We have sometimes added further information if it was needed and available—which it often was not.

This publication, prepared in the Office of Educational Programs under Assistant Archivist Albert Meisel and Barbara Shissler Nosanow, Director of the Education Division, required devotion and long hours from many. I wish particularly to thank Caryl Marsh, Curator of Exhibitions and Research; Christina Rudy, Coordinator of the Exhibition; the Exhibits Staff, Lillian Grandy, Dana Wegner, and Claudia Nicholson; Philip C. Brooks, Jr., Assistant to the Assistant Archivist, who helped with many arduous administrative problems; and volunteers Helen Goldman and Karen Elliott.

Without the generous cooperation of the Audiovisual Archives Division under James W. Moore, and the entire staff of the Still Picture Branch under Joe Thomas, particularly William H. Leary, Barbara Lewis, and Jonathan Heller, this project would not have been possible.

And finally, a special thanks to the others who helped in the preliminary selection of photographs: Nancy E. Malan, Jean Meisel, and docents Audrey Kelly, Jean Rose, Ann Trombley, Lynne Murphy, Ann Bixby, and Donya Platoff.

JAMES B. RHOADS
Archivist of the United States

Introduction: Photographs as Symbolic History

Not long after the birth of photography in 1839 Oliver Wendell Holmes cast a curious eye toward the millions of images already gathering on table-tops and in drawers across America, the countless albums and prints and cards, and wondered what was to come of such an "enormous collection." Writing in the *Atlantic Monthly* in 1859, the noted doctor and philosopher confessed himself enraptured by the new medium, smitten by its uncanny "appearance of reality that cheats the senses with its seeming truth." Photographs were magical illusions. But even more than that, he explained, they were matchless pieces of information, descriptions of things, scenes, and persons infinitely more vivid than words. As if photographs were the very skin or surface of things stripped and preserved, they seemed miniature worlds: not copies, but the things themselves. Eventually, he foresaw, photography would reproduce the entire world, reducing all solid objects to thin film images. Indeed, the time was fast approaching when everything under the sun would be available "for inspection" as images.

That time has long since arrived, and now, almost one hundred and fifty years after the invention of photography, we wonder how the world ever managed its business without it. Photographs have become so thoroughly ingrained in our way of life that we rarely give them a second thought. They seem part of the air we breathe, as natural as language. And very much like language, they frame our world. They show us how things look, how we ourselves look, and often, in advertisements and pictures of celebrities, how we may want to look. Photographs are compelling things, and more than we may want to admit, they fashion and guide our most basic sense of reality.

Writing on the threshold of its career, Holmes anticipated the camera's immense power to shape our world, and this led him to make a remarkable proposal. All those fabulous pictures, he explained, "will have to be classified and arranged in vast libraries, as books are now." Fascinated particularly by the stereograph, which created a three-dimensional effect when viewed in a special holder, he envisioned a library of stereo-cards. But his words ring true, and prophetic, for photography as a whole. "We do now distinctly propose," he wrote, "the creation of a comprehensive and systematic stereograph library, where all men can find the special forms they particularly desire to see as artists, or as scholars, or as mechanics, or in any other capacity."

At least another generation passed before libraries began systematically to collect and classify photographs. But Holmes's proposal, and his enthusiasm, seem notably appropriate as an introduction to this book of photographs culled from one of the world's most important and unique collections. Like the collection Holmes envisioned, the pictures in the holdings of the National Archives touch upon almost everything under the sun, literally from nuts (and fruits) to bolts. But what makes the collection truly extraordinary—as the pictures in this book testify—is its unique ties to American life, to the history of its everyday affairs as much as to the history of its major events and personalities. Here, in this handful of representative pictures, we can see American history made vivid and concrete—vivid, concrete, and dramatic in the special ways of photography. The pictures are examples of one of the nation's major resources for the study of its life, past and present. For photography *is* a resource, as Holmes understood, without precedent and without peer: a special kind of knowledge available to all interested parties. The pictures presented here are documents of history, but they are also experiences in their own right; they offer us a privileged opportunity to witness the past as if it were, momentarily, present. The book is a history lesson of sorts. It is also—and this is very much part of the lesson—an opportunity to think about the special resources and properties of photographs, and of what gives them the power that moved Oliver Wendell Holmes, and a multitude of other commentators, to proclaim a new era in human knowledge.

I

Pictorial histories are certainly not a new phenomenon. For many years, since the invention of efficient half-tone reproduction of photographic images in newspapers and books in the 1890s, editors and writers have combed picture archives for striking and colorful images, either to illustrate history texts, or, as in Frederick Lewis Allen's *American Procession* (1933), to construct a panorama of American life. Recently interest has grown in studying photographs not simply as illustrations of history but also as revealing documents and expressions, as the source of insight as well as information not so readily available in other media. True, Mathew Brady's famous picture of General Sherman "illustrates" his appearance, his uniform, his military decoration—and the black crepe sash tied in a bow above his elbow as the official sign of mourning for the death of President Lincoln. But the picture discloses even more about the grizzle-bearded warrior, stiff and straight in his chair against a plain background. Everyone can recognize the picture as a "portrait," not a candid snapshot, and so we take for granted that Sherman is knowingly *posing*, that he prepared himself for a picture he realizes will represent him, his visage and his image, to the world. True, he has not taken any great pains to brush his hair or straighten his tie; neither he nor Brady wanted especially to show a man too scrupulous about his neatness. Instead, Sherman makes his point about himself by his military posture, by the arms folded with certainty and self-assurance across his chest. His eyes peer off toward the distance: does he mean to show what he looks like on a battlefield, gauging enemy fortifications, or is he in fact in a blank stare? In any case, he is not looking directly into the lens, preferring perhaps to be *looked at* without giving the viewer a feeling that the general is exchanging a glance with the public.

If we look closely at the photograph, as we would at a painting, we see that we can actually *read* the picture, that it reveals more than it merely illustrates. We can reconstruct some small drama, or sequence of happenings before the taking of the picture, that itself tells us more than meets the eye about Sherman, and also something about Brady's willingness to allow the camera to record such a direct, undisguised encounter. In venturing such reconstructions out of photographs, moreover, we begin to reach critical points of difference between camera-made images and those painted or drawn by hand. A painting, for example, tempts and invites us to reconstruct, not a happening which the painting imitates, but some vision and intent of the painter's, something in his mind's eye (even though he may be copying a scene from real life). We involve ourselves differently with photographs. True, we look for personal vision and intention, but also signs of real life. These signs are not always obvious nor are they simple to see and to read. Compare the portrait of Sherman with that of President Roosevelt and Winston Churchill at Marrakech after the Casablanca conference in 1943. The differences are striking, and point not only to different cameras and lenses (the photographer here was obviously able to get closer, in vision if not in body, with a longer lens), but an entirely different relationship between the camera and its subject, and the picture and its viewer. The Brady portrait expresses an era when photographic portraits were almost entirely formal in pose and decorous in style. It is not likely that Brady would photograph a public figure unawares, without his cooperation. The candid picture of the two wartime leaders—a fascinating study in contrasts—presupposes that both the subjects and the viewers of the picture accept the legitimacy and indeed the accuracy of candid, informal pictures of public figures. The picture conveys a kind of intimacy with person and scene simply not true of Brady's portraits: like a movie close-up, the picture gives us the illusion of being invisibly present as emotion unfolds. We feel such images are somehow more "real" because more "immediate" than the studied composures of face and body in Brady's pictures. *(See pp. 58, 172.)*

Such differences among pictures made at different moments in history are instructive, for they reveal how powerfully photography is influenced by prevailing assumptions about pictures of all kinds, and about such subjects as the proper appearance of a public figure. Of course the rapid development of photography as the predominant visual medium of communication itself influenced these assumptions, giving to the image a power over ideas of "truth" and "reality" never possessed by any other medium. But truth and reality are relative terms. Compare, for example, typical photographs made during the Civil War with those made in the two twentieth-century World Wars. What did the photographer intend in the picture of the *Chickamauga*? Merely to show an Army transport being loaded somewhere along the Tennessee River? Or does the positioning of the camera at a site above the scene, distant enough for us to have a whole view of all the sundry activities, give us, the viewers, a particular role to play? The elevated perspective makes the scene a vista. An "overall, distant view of things dominates" in the Brady Civil War pictures, as Joel Snyder accurately points out, a view which corresponds to the theory implicit in most photographic practice at the time: that the camera was like the eye of eternity.[1] Every event had its place in a comprehensible scheme of things. The loading of the *Chickamauga* was worthy of depiction because it fit a larger unfolding story. Positioned on that elevation, the viewer is like a detached, though interested, audience of a drama. The eye-level perspective of the group portrait, "Section of Keystone Battery," serves a similar function. The group is placed in middle-distance, as if on a stage before the viewer, and the men position themselves in a manner part formal, part casual, as if before an audience. As the "Keystone Battery" they are performing a role, albeit a small one, in a destiny. The contrast with typical twentieth-century war scenes could hardly be more stark. Here, as Snyder points out, the photographer seems to be "in the center of the action." The soldiers—the 23rd Infantry gun crew in World War I, "U.S. Marines pinned down on Peliliu" in World War II—are oblivious to the camera, just as, for the viewer, they are rather blurred images of figures and movement, not distinct individuals. Action—and its spontaneous and authentic representation (often entailing blurs and slanted angles)—seems the essence of these pictures, not destiny. Changes in the photographic image of war follow changes in the very conception of war, of the individual's role within it, and the role of the home-front viewer. *(See pp. 21, 19, 105, 167.)*

A photographic history lesson, then, must first awaken in the viewer a sensitivity to the *language* of photography—or the several languages—for a variety of styles, of methods, of functions abound in the history of the medium. And a rich assortment of kinds of pictures along with a fascinating range of subjects confront the viewer and invite his close attention in this selection from the National Archives. Of course photographs give pleasure as well as history lessons, and among these photographs we find many that are simply beautiful to look at, to contemplate and muse over. But the particular point of this group of pictures is to open a path from the present to the past, to bring the past into our present lives with the vividness, immediacy, and gripping concreteness that photographs make possible.

The photographs collected by the National Archives are especially appropriate as a source for such

a lesson in reading history. By and large photographs appear in the Archives only if they have already served some purpose linked to "history,"—that is, if they have been part of the work of a government agency. There are exceptions, of course—the Brady Collection is the most notable—but on the whole the Archives photographs represent documents accumulated in the course of government work. Pictures are not collected for their aesthetic importance, nor because they represent significant moments in the history of photography. They are collected simply because they once played a useful function. The mission of the National Archives (founded in 1934) is to provide a place for records no longer in active use—to keep, preserve, and make available "the experience of the Government and people of the United States as it is embodied in records of the Federal Government and related materials." A somewhat fuller statement in the *Guide to the National Archives of the United States* (1974) explains that the material it holds "was originally created or received by legislative, judicial, or executive agencies of the Government in pursuance of their legal obligations or in the transaction of their official business. This material was maintained by these agencies as an official record of their activities or because of the value of the information it contained."[2]

The Archives gives the impression of a virtually bottomless repository of historical memory. It keeps, and displays, documents sacred to the nation's memory, such as the Declaration of Independence and the Constitution, and also items that might strike the casual browser as the most trivial and incidental of records of government operations. Everything is organized according to "record group," each containing the papers of a particular agency or bureau—papers that have outlived their original purpose and are now transformed, as it were, into "history." Of course such records are simply inert facts or objects until they are brought to life again by some new use, a new purpose. "Past is Prologue" is the motto of the National Archives, and the *Guide* is like the map of a forgotten terrain, a systematic key to that portion of the past that lies within the domain of government work—or that part of the past created by the activities of government. The latest *Guide* lists 409 "record groups," the number hinting at the size and range of government domain. And what one is likely to find in that domain, what records and what details of American history, is often quite surprising.

As for photographs, they are often among the most pleasant and disarming of surprises. It is actually an advantage, for a variety of reasons, that photographs belong to the Archives by virtue of their historical rather than aesthetic value. This is not to say that many of the photographs, such as those selected for this book, are not interesting simply for their visual pleasure. The landscape photographs included here by Timothy O'Sullivan, Jack Hillers, and Carleton Watkins are among the acclaimed masterpieces of the art of photography, and the collection includes distinguished pictures by many other figures accepted as artists in the medium of photography (Mathew Brady, George Barnard, William Henry Jackson, Lewis Hine, Edward Steichen, Dorothea Lange, Russell Lee, and Ansel Adams among others). But the opportunity to see famous and lovely pictures in the context of other pictures—less interesting in form or visual excitement—heightens the surprise we feel in discovering that a beautiful picture may also have a specific, valuable, historical meaning embedded within its value as an aesthetic experience. All photographs—the great, the merely interesting, the commonplace—have a place in the Archives only as they fall within a "record group" (including the miscellaneous group called "Gift Collection"), only as they relate *in some fashion* to a government activity. Usually they are filed under a specific subject matter within a "record group"; rarely are they filed by the name of the photographer (a practice widely at variance with that of "art" collections). The surprises that await the researcher often lie in finding pictures that seem only tangentially connected to any imaginable function of a particular agency—or, often enough, not connected at all in any apparent way. Sometimes verbal documentation can be found explaining why a particular picture was deposited within a particular "record group," but such information cannot always be counted on.

In what sense is this situation, anomalous among archives of art works, an "advantage"? Partly because it leads to an extraordinary feeling of adventure, which staff members of the Audiovisual Archives Division and other researchers often feel. And partly because it compels the researcher and viewer to confront pictures directly, head-on, from the point of view of their meaning and value as historical documents. If they are also strong pictures from a strictly visual point of view, so much the better; their value as documents is then enhanced. A stronger picture will invite a closer inspection, a more detailed analysis, a deeper involvement on the part of viewer. Most likely he will feel compelled to think about the information in the picture along with the *form* by which the picture informs—to think, that is, about the connections between aesthetics and history.

Such connections are, of course, often the subject of fierce controversy among scholars and critics in the field of art. Some art historians insist upon a separation of the form of a work of art from its content, from the story or scene or person it represents. From this point of view the circumstances under which a painting was created, its relation to the biography of the artist, the influence of the historical moment, are incidental concerns, important only as they illuminate the picture and enhance our appreciation of it as an art work. In most photographs the content or subject matter is so prominent—it is, of course, what we initially look at and see—that a separation of form and content often seems unnecessary, or a barren exercise. The connection between a photograph and its subject seems so immediate, so certain, so inevitable, that form and content appear as one. Perhaps for this reason, and also because of the high degree of mechanical or automatic procedure in the making of a photograph, art histories have tended, until recently, to ignore photographs, to exclude them from the variety of visual expressions that qualify as "art" worth looking at and thinking about as significant experiences. Very often photographs have been relegated by art historians (whose own books, by the way, rely heavily on photographic reproductions of paintings or images of sculpture and architecture), and also by general historians, to the status of illustrations, or visual examples of a certain subject matter.

By filing photographs under "record groups" rather than by photographer or by subject, the National Archives collection makes it equally difficult to take the photograph either as simply an illustration of a subject or as purely an aesthetic object. Of course anybody can take either point of view, or any other, toward any picture. But the particular *form* of the Archives collection does invite an experience of pictures without preconceptions. If one looks, for example, among the 75,089 photographs listed within the records of the Bureau of Reclamation to find pictures that effectively describe or recount aspects of American life—as did the staff members who prepared the selections for this book—what is one likely to find? The results are surprising, and revealing. Bureau activities included power and irrigation projects throughout the West, and projects concerned with "roads, bridges, rivers, floods, drought conditions" in the West and South. Researchers found a group of pictures made in the Far West and Southwest between 1905 and 1908 by W. J. Lubken, presumably a staff photographer for the Bureau, and several others by other hands. The explicit subjects in most cases do indeed seem related to Bureau activities: two men operating an "Ingersoll drill" in a "diversion channel" project, a newly completed dam, a reservoir, a group of trappers and hunters, a fisherman, a government automobile. The most overt illustrative level—probably the chief reason each picture was taken—is only the beginning, however, of the experience of these wonderfully evocative pictures. They evoke a host of additional perceptions, recognitions, provocations of curiosity, incitements to thought. The "native fisherman of the Colorado River, fishing in the Imperial Canal" shows a man in a wet loin cloth and shirt standing barefooted on the rocky bank of a stream from which he may have just emerged with his equipment—a net hung between two rough-hewn poles. He looks directly at the camera, in a position of pause and attention we recognize as a "pose." It seems obvious he would not take such a position unless a photographer had wandered along and asked him to hold still. The question is, what is the photographer doing? Why did he want or need a picture of a man and a method of fishing that virtually everyone likely to see the picture would call "primitive"? Was the Imperial Canal designed with the needs of such fishermen in mind, in which case does the picture "say" that the purpose of the construction is being fulfilled? Or can we take the rubble on the banks of the stream to suggest that the construction of the canal is still in progress, that the fisherman is not so

much fishing in a government-made canal but in what he might consider native waters, and thus that the picture is meant to mean something like "transition," "an image of old ways passing out of existence"? Perhaps deep in the records of the Bureau there rests a written document that answers such questions, or proves them irrelevant and foolish. Without such documentation we are intrigued, perhaps baffled, but certainly engaged by the picture and its possible implications. *(See pp. 97, 35.)*

Take all of the Bureau of Reclamation pictures included here as a separate group, just for the moment, and the image of the "native fisherman" takes on even more suggestions as a *contrast* to the government work of changing and controlling the shape of the land. A contrast is pointed and urged upon us simply by the form of the fisherman picture and that of the Ingersoll drill, which, as a power-driven tool, takes entirely different kinds of muscular exertion and control than does the fisherman's net, and imposes a different relation between itself and its human manipulator, a difference in physical tension and finally in the basic relation (which include emotions) between man and his tools. The drill picture has provocations in its own right: mainly a picture of a man at work, it is probably a picture of a man posing *as if* he were at work. In operation the drill would certainly be in motion and it and the worker would leave only a blur on the photographic film. The glance of the seated figure toward the camera is a key that both men are aware of the presence of a camera. Moreover, it appears that another camera is stationed in the picture—though out of range of clear focus—in the left-center middle-ground (standing on a tripod): an extremely incidental detail, but one which suggests a larger theme, that the presence of a photographer often disrupts and modifies a scene, making it over into a *photographed* scene. The photographer's intervention results in a scene that is not quite "true," not quite "reality" as it is lived, with all its complexity and unpredictableness, but yet bears some close relation to that "reality," close enough for us to take the picture without serious question as a fairly reliable image of what did exist. Still, the question arises and persists: How much of the picture belongs to the photographer's arrangement, how much to any sitter's collaboration, and how much simply to the scene as it was in fact?

One final example from this group. "Raising and lowering gates at newly completed diversion dam at head of main Truckee canal on Truckee River at the opening of the Truckee-Carson project" is, like its caption, a picture with more in it than the previous two. The others can be usefully described as "portraits"—a term taken from painting and indicating one of the large areas in which photography has followed the lead of older media of representation—in that they concentrate on single figures (two in the case of the drill picture) who, while relatively informal in their postures, do take notice of the photographer and pose for him. This picture is obviously entirely different. It is a view from a distance of both a structure and an event (or many small events) that sprawls across it: the opening of the dam gates together with the activity of watching the event (and even, along the lower left-hand corner, photographing it). The photographer is not looking at single individuals, who seem oblivious of him. He is at a distance, on a rise—like the Civil War photographer who took the picture of the *Chickamauga*—taking in the scene as if he were detached from it, a mere observer. Thus the picture seems merely to illustrate an event within a scene. *(See p. 98.)*

But in fact the picture shows more than the event itself, more even than the dam's structure, which is also part of the documentary interest of the picture. The structure and the activities occurring on and around it occupy not much more than the lower half of the picture. The rest is given over to space, a spreading flat plain that reaches to the base of a range of mountains that in turn rises in curves and slopes, virtually billowing to the top of the picture frame. We realize that this upper section of the picture is there because the photographer meant it to be, and moreover, that he has placed his camera in such a way that the lines in the actual terrain can be seen from such an angle, in such a perspective, that our eye

is guided toward the elevation in the distance. We realize, in short, that the picture has been *composed* rather carefully and artfully, that the happenings around the dam have been placed within a landscape, and that the landscape in turn gives us yet another perspective upon the main event. Perhaps the intention was to enhance the event by showing it in a setting of grandeur. Moreover, the setting itself is curiously and intriguingly reflected in the structure of the dam, its curves and slopes, its pillars and arches repeating shapes that we see in the mountains. We might begin to see the entire picture in strictly formal terms, a disposition of lines and shapes, an interesting geometric design emerging from the literal details of the scene. But the picture remains literal, as its cumbersome caption reminds us, and returning to its subject matter after thinking about its abstract form, we can then recognize ways that the form contributes to the subject, clarifies not only what it is—an opening ceremony of a construction project within the wide spaces of the Far West—but also its meanings. The relation of diagonals to curves, for example, might be taken as the *form* of the relation of the mechanical to the natural, between the work of human technology (dam and railroad streaking along the straight horizontal path at the base of the mountains, and also cameras) and the work of natural time (the patterns of erosion in the distant hills). The human forms seem to half imitate the natural forms, only leveling them out, straightening their bumps and irregularities into machine-made lines. And meanwhile the people themselves, in their variety of postures (see the marvelous lines of characters stationed at the gates above the pillars on the left), occupy a middle range of regularity and irregularity, nature and civilization, between the two poles of the absolutely natural and the absolutely mechanical.

The picture, then, holds a provoking subject matter in a tense relation to a compositional design, and we are left wondering if W. J. Lubken, staff photographer for the Bureau of Reclamation on assignment to make a record of a ceremony, had all this in mind when he placed his camera where he did—or if it matters whether he saw and intended everything we see. For the picture documents certain implicit ideas of both a disruption between man and nature, and a subtle continuity with nature in the forms of man's buildings, as much as it documents a specific event. And those implicit ideas are as authentic and valid data of history as the literal dam itself.

II

Not without cause, people are more prone to "believe" a photograph than they are a painting or a drawing. This trust, of course, is often naïve; the camera *can* lie as often and as cleverly as any other tool wielded by people intent on telling lies. And even in the best of cases, where the photographer is as honest as one can wish, his picture will inevitably show only what the particular lens on the camera is capable of showing, in the way of depth, clarity, and spatial relations. The very frame of the photograph is itself something of a distortion or imposition; had we been present at the scene, standing where the camera stood, we all know that we would have seen more than what the frame allows us to see. Cropping of a scene cuts off the viewer from other details that may well be relevant to an understanding of the picture. This is, to be sure, obvious and commonplace. But these inherent limitations in the truth-telling capacities of photography point to one of its essential characteristics, and one of its major differences from paintings and drawings: the picture could not have been made had not a camera been present at the scene of its making. Photographs cannot be made from memory. A photographer does not retire to a studio to render a scene he has witnessed; he makes the rendering at the same time that he witnesses the scene. Of course many artists also paint or draw before a living scene, either a person or an object or a view. But the camera makes its exposure and its record on film instantaneously. The photographer has considerable leeway in the darkroom to alter tones and to crop even further; he may also retouch or manipulate the image in other ways. But when he does so he is altering a picture that already exists: the picture formed in the chemical changes on emulsified film in the fraction of a second measured by the click of the shutter. Any straight, single-negative photograph tells us that at the very least a camera was *there*, where something happened.

Simply as a property of the technique of the medium, a photograph lends a special kind of *presence* to what it depicts, quite decidedly different from the presence of objects, persons, or places one feels before a painting. Every unaltered photograph is a record of time past. We may look at the picture as timeless, but a closer look will usually betray the sign of a specific happening present to the lens at a specific time. O'Sullivan's monumental picture of the ruins at Canyon de Chelly is an excellent example. Look closely, and you will notice four inconspicuous human figures, members of the photographer's

party, in various postures among the ruins; one figure, low in the left-hand corner, holds the scaling ropes by which the two men looking toward the camera mounted the highest ruins. What is the photograph a picture *of*? The four figures, the ropes, the signs of an exploration party? All these small items need to be included in any answer. They give to the picture the presence proper to a photographic record of a definite moment in time and space. Of course painters often attempt and achieve a similar kind of specificity of time and place. But what is present to the viewer of a canvas is not so much the action of light recording itself as it falls on film, but the rendering of a vision in the eyes and mind of an artist, whose hands and fingers are skilled enough to make the vision clear and palpable for others. The painting refers back to the artist as its origins; the photograph points both to the camera and to the scene in its field of vision. *(See p. 34.)*

Then is the photographer himself of no real importance? It runs deeply against the grain of our convictions to say so. Yet in one very limited sense it is true. Anyone can make a photograph. And any photograph, as dull or as unfocused, or as conventional as it may be, will have its points of interest. That interest, as an astute Englishwoman, Lady Elizabeth Eastlake, put it as early as the 1850s, is "historic":

> Every form which is traced by light is the impress of one moment, or one hour, or one age in the great passage of time. Though the faces of our children may not be modelled and rounded with that truth and beauty which art attains, yet minor things—the very shoes of the one, the inseparable toy of the other—are given with a strength of identity which art does not even seek. Though the view of a city be deficient in those niceties of reflected lights and harmonious gradations which belong to the facts of which Art takes account, yet the facts of the age and of the hour are there, for we count the lines in that keen perspective of telegraphic wire, and read the characters on that playbill or manifesto, destined to be torn down on the morrow.[3]

Lady Eastlake speaks in effect of snapshots, and can her argument be denied? Because of its special mode of endowing its image with presence, as if by automatic action, the photograph is a unique historical record, one that allows us to read, to count, even to measure what once existed.

From this point of view, simply of what can be measured, what facts and details identified and counted, the group of pictures presented here have an unmistakable historical value. Here we can see, in vivid detail, almost as if we had been present, scenes from the familiar passages of American history in the hundred years between 1860 and 1960: the battlefields of three wars, the faces of many famous Americans, the Western landscape as it appeared to government survey and exploration expeditions in the 1870s, frontier settlements, Native Americans both in their own settlements and in photographers' studios in their full get-ups, men, women and children in factories, people at picnics or in living rooms, and so on. War, exploration and settlement, rise of the city, mechanization, immigration, racial conflict: these and other of the major themes by which historians have tracked the history of these years can all find some visual evidence—perhaps visual equivalents—in these pictures. And even in this limited

light, as sheer documents of the look of things, these pictures also add something to our historical knowledge. The past is always immeasurably more complex than any written narrative can suggest. Because of the particular way photographs are made—by the action of light—they record small details of the sort usually ignored (if only for efficiency's sake) by historians: precisely what kind of clothing—hats, shirts, suspenders—were worn by "Negro laborers" as they are shown in the Brady picture, and what kinds of facial expressions they are likely to put on when asked to pose as a group before a photographer; what General Martin T. McMahon and his staff thought of themselves and their image as warriors, as heroes, as best we can tell from their postures and their appearances in the group portrait made just after the Civil War; or what we can read of the complicated situation of Native Americans in the 1870s from the differences in how they present themselves to the camera between O'Sullivan's "Navaho Group" at their own dwelling, and Will Soule's "Navajo Silversmith," taken in the same years; or what life was like for "convalescent officers" in World War I ("Mrs. W. E. Corey playing cards with wounded officers on the porch"), and for wounded soldiers ("The American Advance in the Argonne"); or what difference radio made in the way a family gathered in the living room down on the farm ("Sometimes the whole family gathered around the receiving set"), and then the difference of television, in the age of media images (note the photographs on the wall, and how the TV image holds all members of the family equally, in "A family watches a debate between John F. Kennedy and Richard Nixon"). *(See pp. 9, 24, 35, 60, 108, 106.)*

To be sure, there is much more to reading a photograph than recognizing its details and connecting what they show with a larger frame or scheme—in this case, our common knowledge of American

history—and we will have to confront that "more" shortly. But it is worthwhile to continue in this vein a bit further, for this particular group of pictures, taken as a whole (rather than as single expressive images), does make a significant addition to historical knowledge simply on the level of what is represented. The pictures document a changing society, and they do so, much more than is the case in most history textbooks, from the point of view of people who experienced change: not only the children working in a coal mine, crammed into a tight space for a photograph by Lewis Hine, but the families tuned in to radio and television. There is still a conviction, though it may be changing, that history is made by leaders and governments, by larger-than-life heroes and villains—and that plain people only live in their wake. The thematic emphasis in these pictures is upon plain people, and especially upon people engaged in work. Work, physical labor, is a powerfully recurring motif here. The sequence of pictures opens with views of monumental and symbolic buildings in construction, and this theme of construction runs throughout, counterpointed by scenes of ruin and devastation in warfare. Think of the variety of kinds of work displayed here; we see explorers, sailors, hunters, prospectors, farmers, miners, soldiers, teamsters, cowboys, convict laborers; we see women in factories and on farms, and children in mines and mills as well as schools. Simply as visual fact, this particular photographic history underlines the presence of working people in our history. It also underlines the fact, until recently blocked from the consciousness of many white Americans, that ours is a multiracial population, that blacks and Indians and Asians share an American identity just as they share (as many of the photographs reveal) work and play. *(See pp. 184, 131, 96.)*

Taken as a single ensemble of views of American people and places, a stitched-together panorama, the pictures can tease us into a kind of interpretation we might give to a work of literature. We might, as our imaginations play over the sequence, pick out certain motifs, watch them develop, reappear, fuse with other motifs and images, and coalesce in our minds into a new insight. Take the various images of

natural terrain, of what, as an idea, we call "nature." They range from the swamp and ruminating cows in the foreground of a scene which rises toward the Capitol dome, to the solemn Cathedral Spires of Yosemite and the cavernous gulches and strata of erosion in the Grand Canyon—both rendered by the photographer as "landscapes" following painterly compositions in organizing their views. An enduring idea that flourished especially among painters and poets and clergymen in the nineteenth century, and persists still, is that America has a special affinity with "nature," that the country is in a sense "God's country." Surely many viewers will look upon the Western landscape photographs in this light. The scale of the pictured landscape among the canyons and rock formations and giant trees of the West is awesome; human figures are dwarfed yet often seem in peaceful harmony with the natural setting. For viewers so disposed these particular pictures might well support a religious or an aesthetic view of nature, in which the terrain of rocks and sky and vegetation and water is an inspiration, perhaps a solace. Another point of view might see the open spaces of the plains, the Rockies and beyond, as many Americans did in the nineteenth century, as beckoning the new society forward, toward a "manifest destiny," an American empire in the West. It seems likely that many of the photographers themselves entertained one or all of these cultural outlooks. *(See pp. 1, 30, 27.)*

But whatever fancy these pictures evoke in us, seen within this particular sequence of images, they dramatize the overriding *fact* of a particular natural terrain within which American history occurs: "nature," that is as geography, issuing its own imperatives and having its own say in shaping human

actions. The mountains, rivers, canyons, prairies, deserts, are not only capable of serving as symbols (religious, aesthetic, or philosophical), but they are also real places in a human historical enterprise. This may in fact be a buried point in one of the most stunning and moving of the pictures in the group, O'Sullivan's famous photograph of his wagon darkroom in the Carson Desert, Nevada. The power of the picture lies in its apparent simplicity: the dark forms of the wagon and team of mules against the light sand dunes behind, bordered at either edge by darker forms etched against a bright noon sky, indicated by the position of the shadows under the mules and wagon. O'Sullivan often depicted stark edges of rock formation and receding planes of sloping hills against the sky. In general his pictures among the Western photographs seem the least conventionally composed, the most attuned to the drama of line, shape, texture, and light that the camera itself can detect or elicit and record. Here he seems to want to show no more than the presence of his wagon within such an empty, inhuman, and with the desert heat we can assume, threatening setting. But showing that, and the footsteps that seem to lead from the wagon toward the camera position, he achieves something more, a symbolic statement that reflects upon the entire enterprise of exploring and surveying the western lands, and making photographs of their wild, unexpected natural forms. For the wagon and the footsteps are signs of his own presence in this scene, a presence that disrupts the perfect *natural* harmony of the scene, that in effect ruptures the idea that the photographer's subject is a pure, unspoiled, and unsullied nature. The picture is rich with suggestion: Are these the sands of time that will before long efface the tracks of man, just as the imposing rocks and mountains in other pictures might be taken as silent sentinels, reminders that the land itself has a natural history that far exceeds America's? But one suggestion that wins support by its echo in other pictures is that the wagon represents not only "man," but a particular kind of work—the work most prominent in the entire group of pictures—that of the photographer himself. In its simplicities of contrast the picture seems to factualize "nature," to remove it from mystery and place it within the range of experiences capable of being photographed, an act, the picture seems to say, which subtly modifies the natural, transforms it for human consumption. The wagon not only measures the scale of the hill of sand, but it also makes that hill available to our comprehension. We no longer have a "landscape" with its associations of devotion, reverence, sublime emotion. Instead, we have the land in one of its most barren forms, and a photographer: and in the transaction between them, an image that might serve as a symbol of the complex relations between man and land, society and geography, that runs throughout American history. *(See p. 33.)*

(See p. 33.)

III

O'Sullivan's wagon darkroom picture takes us swiftly from a discussion of the literal content of the photographs to their symbolic suggestions. In reading pictures as symbols—and we do this with paintings as well as photographs—we try to get inside the mind of the artist, to ferret out his intentions, or to point out ways in which his picture may say even more than he realized or intended. But symbolic interpretation is an enterprise full of risks, not least of which is the temptation to be reckless, to venture guesses without evidence. Like all pictures photographs invite interpretations, but the interpreter needs some controls upon his own imagination, some limits and a boundary between sense and non-sense. Where are they to be found, and where placed?

The problem of interpreting photographs is like the proverbial can of worms. It is hard to get a solid hold on it. Of all the modes of visual expression the photograph is perhaps the least understood, the least commonly agreed upon. There is little help to be found in the kinds of strictly formal analyses appropriate to paintings, though some awareness of the effect of lines and relations of shapes and tones is essential. Formal analysis, moreover, tends to confine the photograph to a narrow range of meanings. It cannot do justice to the special relationship that exists in the photograph between its form and its content, a relationship based on the photographic presence already discussed. And it adds little to the question that interested Oliver Wendell Holmes: What is special, what is different, about photographs as *knowledge* of the world? What can we *know* through a photograph that cannot be known in any other way?

It may well be that the question is unanswerable, or that a simple answer is "nothing"—that is, that photographs are really not unique either as pictures or knowledge. But writers on photography have suggested some positive answers, and one in particular seems at least useful enough for this selection from the National Archives to warrant a brief discussion. That is, to see photographs not so much as formal pictures but as events, actions, performances, communications. The principle is to recognize that the meaning of a photograph—what the interpreter is after—is rarely a given within the picture, but is developed in the *function* of the picture, in its particular social use by particular people. Photographs have a multitude of uses, some private, some public, and we can take each use as its context or (to borrow a term from the sociologist Erving Goffman) "frame."[4] A baby picture in the frame of private consumption by mother, father, grandparents, is a different picture from the very same image examined by a doctor for evidence of skin eruptions or malstructure, or by a photo-historian as an example of a popular genre. Change the frame, and the meaning also changes, though the image remains the same. Of course the same can be said of all pictures, but in fact paintings are usually already framed, literally, and set aside from commonplace experience as "art," properly viewed on a wall. Photographs have simply developed a far wider range of social functions, and are thus that much more difficult to pin down to a single definition.

One of the common features of the pictures shown here is that we have by and large lost the original frames. The "record group" location of the National Archives photographs, as we have seen, is only haphazardly helpful in reconstructing that frame, and thus in recovering an original meaning. Internal evidence sometimes helps, especially in studio portraits, where the picture is often itself a clear record of a collaboration and an intention. But internal evidence alone is not fully reliable. Was the picture published, and if so, where? Assuming that most of the National Archives photographs were produced as public communications, not as tokens of private transactions within families or among friends, the missing frame is likely to represent some communication within a definite social scene. Captions usually identify subject matter and photographer, but not the scene in which the photograph was meant to play a role. Clearly, much more verbal documentation is wanted if we wish to reconstruct all the original purposes, contexts, and frames of these pictures. Such a reconstruction would take a monumental task of research, and its results would add invaluable new knowledge about the history of American life, its many small patterns of interaction, its changing modes of exchange and communication among people. For photography is a form of behavior—or many forms, each bearing important information about the daily lives of Americans, about those expectations and implicit values that make up the everyday life of any society. This is to say that the historical and documentary value of these photographs does not lie wholly in their visual subject matter—in what they are as recorded perceptions—but also in the buried and hidden social uses they originally performed. Each picture presented here, then, represents more than itself: each is a symbol of meanings, of frameworks within which the picture performed its original work, that in turn lead as if by infinite regress into the patterns, values, and beliefs of American culture at any given moment of its history.

To explicate the "meaning" of each picture in this archaeological sense is, to be sure, a hopeless task. We need far more detailed information about how photographers worked, about their relations of obligation and commercial arrangement with clients, their ways of presenting pictures to particular audiences, particular publics. We need to know much more than we do about how people behaved toward such "public" pictures (leaving aside the even more intricate matter of the private use of photographs within families), whether they preserved them, hung them (and where), inscribed them in memory, or whatever. The photographs we see here are surely an enormous enrichment of our historical knowledge, let alone our visual pleasure, but they also remind us how impoverished we are in many regions of knowledge, especially in the history of common, everyday life. And that reminder can lead us back to the pictures themselves, perhaps with an added hunger for more information, more detail, more clarity of purpose and meaning.

Recognizing how much more we need to know in order to know perfectly the meaning of the pictures, we can then begin to ask leading questions, to construct frames of our own for the use and appreciation of these images. Our questions may be aesthetic, or art-historical, or political, or broadly historical and cultural. We can take O'Sullivan's "wagon darkroom" as a marvelous design in form (which it is), a sign of the individual talent of this extraordinary photographer, and a sign too of a phase in the history of photography (the use of wet-plate equipment for open-air work). It is all of this, and all such questions are legitimate. It is also, as we have seen, a thoughtful statement about man and nature, the West, and also about photography; on this level of idea its interest is very much historical and cultural. It comments upon a particular moment in a changing way of life. When we "frame" it culturally, with questions drawn from our own interests in the history of American life, it discloses new possibilities of meaning, without neglecting or disturbing the questions of aesthetics and photographic history.

But a counter-question might arise: Were not Timothy O'Sullivan, Mr. Lubken of the Bureau of Reclamation, and the dozens of others whose pictures appear here really just *working* photographers, craftsmen of the camera, doing the best job they could on particular assignments? Of course. Very few, if any, thought of themselves as "artists," producing pictures for display in "art" exhibitions. Their work was to record a specific scene or event. Primarily their work is straightforward, honest, accurate. They show what their client—often the government—wanted to see and have shown to a public. The purposes of government photography were varied, and precise. They included, as archivist Joe D. Thomas explains, efforts "to supplement the written record of exploration with visual information." And education: "to increase the public's knowledge of their national resources, as in photographs taken by the National Park Service and the Forest Service." Identification is another purpose, of military personnel and military materials, of farm products and the results of agricultural experiment. Documentation of the construction of government buildings is yet another separate category. The reader will easily recognize pictures in this selection which obviously served each of these general functions. Yes, the photographers were first and foremost craftsmen of documentation. But it is because they did their jobs so well, with so little attention to extrinsic and secondary matters of formal aesthetics, that their pictures survive their first purpose and can now serve additional purposes within our own frame of reference. It is because they were so good as photographers that their work is so good now as historical pictures.

The explanation of this residual power and usefulness goes back to one of the fundamental properties of photography, a property that so impressed Oliver Wendell Holmes, Lady Eastlake, and others: its capacity to represent what was *there*. Or, to put it differently, its inability not to show what appears to the lens. A photograph is a record of a past event. It also makes that past moment seem present, here and now: it makes the past present to us, and makes us, as it were, present to the past. It is a complex psychological relationship, as anyone who keeps family photographs in albums or shoe cartons realizes.

A painting, of course, is in some measure *always* here and now; its "past" is the imagination of the painter, not real light rays that once passed through a lens onto a plate or film. A painting may be a *rendering* of a past moment—like John Trumbull's famous conception of the signing of the Declaration of Independence. But it cannot be a direct, physical *impression* of the actual light bouncing off the surfaces of that event. An honest, straight photograph cannot help but put us in touch with history in a manner unique to itself. *(See p. 183.)*

Photographs give immediate access to a past. Thus they make vivid and near-at-hand what written history is about. At the same time, as we have seen, the immediacy is always qualified in some way, in some manner often hidden from us. We can usually tell at a glance what a photograph is about. But the image does not always tell us everything we want to know about it. Viewers of photographs are in a position akin to Helen Keller's in her pictured meeting with President Eisenhower, grasping by touch what she cannot hear. We need to read by interpretation, not by sight alone. And photographs differ yet again from painted or hand-drawn images in that intelligent reading usually begins by looking *through* the picture before looking *at* it. That is, we normally bring to a photograph the skills we have learned in our own everyday lives to recognize gestures, appearances, the signs whereby people and objects signal their functions and intentions to us in real life. Photographs may help us realize, in fact, how much we rely in real life upon acts of *picturing*, of presenting ourselves to others in prepared ways, ways appropriate to certain situations. Every person posing in these photographs is in effect the maker and manipulator of a picture, which the camera then records as a picture *of* a picture. This relationship is quite plain in those photographs of theatrical performance, like "Elsie Ferguson in 'The Spirit That Wins'," or the still from the Liberty Loan film, "Stake Uncle Sam to Play Your Hand," or in the astonishing picture of the "64th Depot Brigade, Camp Funston, Kansas," at once a mass portrait, and a picture made *of* a picture already made by the formation of the brigade into the figure of a banner holding a single star. But some

degree of theatricality, of performance, appears in most pictures of people. Such self-authored images as that of the "forest service ranger" showing off his bear skins and guns, and the three men calling attention to their skills and their luck in capturing the "amazing 'Short-nosed sturgeon'," contain obvious keys to the performance: the trophy defines the character. And the camera defines the stage—or, it provides the opportunity for the performance, just as the photographic process defines its first object or reason: the production of a physical object that will give the performance a certain permanence, making it available for future reference. The performed roles are pretty clear in these pictures, as in the studio portraits of "unidentified Indians from Southeastern Idaho Reservations." But where the presence of the camera does not elicit a complete studiolike decorum—William Henry Jackson's "a group of all the members of the survey made while camping in Red Buttes," for instance—roles are not so clear. In the Jackson example, some figures seem aware of the camera and adjust their positions accordingly; others seem oblivious, and appear as if "caught" in an action that would have occurred even if the camera were not present. Scenes of people at work in factories, in the Mint, in fields, are of this sort, and it is impossible there to make out any specific response. Still, it is evident (and this is one of the ideas so brilliantly clear in O'Sullivan's Carson Desert picture) that one way or another, by posing or framing (cropping) or actually rearranging, the camera itself makes a difference; it too, as an apparatus as well as a photographer's intention, is part of the picture. For this reason, the past we are given access to is not a "pure" objective truth, but a truth already processed and reprocessed by human intention and mechanical limitation. *(See pp. 109, 111, 112, 40, 82, 54, 55, 56, 28.)*

IV

We see, then, that photographs are complicated, difficult objects: complicated by their social functions, made difficult by a relation to the world that is both clear and obscure, simultaneously transparent and opaque. Like miniature replicas, they give us worlds to ponder and amaze ourselves with. They trap our attention and often lead us to bafflement, to mystery. "Son of Clabe Hicks, miner," in

the picture by Russell Lee, may well be a good, sweet, innocent child. The picture is part of a series documenting conditions in West Virginia coal mining regions. Framed as he is in the curtained doorway, the kitchen table behind him (is the meal set, or has it ended?)—framed too by the flowered wallpaper, the domestic photograph of dog and litter above the door, the wonderfully protective slogans tacked on either side ("You Can't Do Wrong and Get By"; "God Bless Our Soldier Boys so Brave and True")—the boy's strangely inexpressive face and his gun (is it a toy? is it loaded?) make a picture of consummate ambiguity. It is a picture *made* of materials that were there, and the making of it condenses those materials into a powerful statement that involves us on several levels, driving us toward questions about Bradshaw, McDowell County, West Virginia, on August 27, 1946—and further, into the corners and shadows of the culture represented by such slogans, such wallpaper, such objects as guns (toy or real) found in the hands of children. *(See p. 153.)*

What are we to make, in a remarkable instance of mysteriousness, of a lost frame, of the picture captioned "Meridian Hill Park. View showing texture of concrete in lower wall. Maid with small children in view"? The caption neglects the tree, or what the wall is doing there, what system of walls it may be part of, and why the texture is worth photographing. The photographer is listed as "unknown," but surely the way he treated this assignment gives him as clear and potent a presence as one can hope for. There are other ways to photograph textures of concrete. But the photographer also saw something else—what appears to be a small drama in process, a visual drama in whites and blacks—as well as textures of cloth

and of skin—of truly unknown import. Is the picture an accident? Here is an example of an apparent violation of a frame: the assignment of picturing textures for the Office of Public Buildings and Public Parks of the National Capital. But the photographer must have had another meaning in mind, if only "human interest." We appreciate his audacity as much as we puzzle over his intention. *(See p. 91.)*

Like such ambiguous pictures, history itself is also a provocation. Its corridors are also blocked by walls without apparent reason or meaning, its written records also pointing toward unexplained actions. The obscurity into which many photographs plunge their contemporary viewers is very much like the obscurity that challenges the historian to get at the bottom of things. One question gives way to another, and the route toward a reliable truth, about photographs as much as history, lies often through a labyrinth of false leads. What other pictures might have been taken of the same subject at the same time, from a slightly different point of view? What really existed beyond the edge of the picture's border? Every photograph takes its image from a living setting; it is always made at the expense of another image that might have been made by another camera with another eye behind it and another purpose in mind. Reading photographs is an active, gymnastic process, as Walt Whitman said about reading poems. It does not require a special skill, only a special attention and an active curiosity. Unexpected pleasures are one reward. Another is the sense one can achieve of participating in the continual public process of making sense of history, of interpreting the past from the perspective of the present. Hardly simple illustrations, photographs can be framed by judicious questions and made into symbols of lived experience: symbols that illuminate just as they provoke further questions. The National Archives collection is a national public resource of immeasurable value. It provides an opportunity to realize one of the oldest ideals of democracy, of making "everyman an historian."

Alan Trachtenberg

NOTES

1. *The Documentary Photograph as a Work of Art: American Photographs, 1860–1876,* Exhibition Catalogue (University of Chicago, 1976), 17–22.

2. *Guide to the National Archives of the United States* (Washington D.C., 1974), 5–6.

3. *London Quarterly Review* (1857), 241–255 (American edition).

4. Erving Goffman, *Frame Analysis* (Harper and Row, New York, 1974), and *Gender Advertisements* (Harper and Row, New York, 1979).

John K. Hillers. "Scene in Marsh on Anacostia River, Washington, Capitol in distance." About 1882. Records of the Geological Survey (57-PS-233).

Dec. 31st
1857

Photographer unknown. Erecting the dome for the U.S. Capitol, Washington, D.C. Dec. 31, 1857. Records of the Office of the Chief of Engineers (77-F-115-2-2).

2

June 7th 1862.

Lewis Emory Walker. Construction of the Department of the Treasury, Washington, D.C. June 7, 1862. Records of the Public Buildings Service (121-BC-9L).

Photographer unknown. "Washington Monument Foundation," Washington, D.C. Aug. 1879. Strengthening the original foundation of 1848 began again after an interruption of eighteen years. Records of the Public Buildings Service (121-BD-54D).

Photographer unknown. "Washington Monument Foundation," Washington, D.C. 1876. Records of the Public Buildings Service (121-BD-54J).

Photographer unknown. Final construction at cap of the Washington Monument, Washington, D.C. 1884. Records of the Public Buildings Service (121-BF-5A).

5

Photographer unknown. Interior of the partially completed Pension Building, Washington, D.C. Nov. 14, 1885. Records of the Veterans Administration (15-M-16).

Civil War (The Brady Collection)

In 1873, the War Department purchased from the financially troubled pioneer photographer Mathew B. Brady (1822-96) part of his Civil War collection of glass negatives. These became the core of the Brady Collection to which the War Department added pictures by other photographers and military agencies.

Brady Collection. Ruins of Richmond, Va. 1865. Records of the Office of the Chief Signal Officer (111-B-112).

Brady Collection. Magazine wharf, City Point, Va. 1864–65. This was the principal Federal depot on the James River during the Civil War. The wheeled boxes are caissons containing ammunition and accoutrements for artillery pieces. Records of the Office of the Chief Signal Officer (111-B-5514).

Brady Collection. "Negro laborers." On the James River or at Alexandria, Va. Date unknown. Records of the Office of the Chief Signal Officer (111-B-400).

Timothy O'Sullivan from the Brady Collection. "Burial place, Fredericksburg, Va." May 12, 1864. Burying dead from the Wilderness Campaign. Records of the Office of the Chief Signal Officer (111-B-4817).

Brady Collection. Wounded soldier, in a Zouave uniform, receiving water in a deserted camp. Date unknown. Records of the Office of the Chief Signal Officer (111-B-250).

Brady Collection. "Pine Cottage." Soldiers' Winter Quarters. 1861–64. Records of the Office of the Chief Signal Officer (111-B-256).

Brady Collection. Private of the 4th Infantry, Michigan. 1861-64. Records of the Office of the Chief Signal Officer (111-B-5348).

Brady Collection. "Deck of gunboat *Hunchback* on James River." May 5, 1864–Feb. 23, 1865. Originally a New York City ferryboat, the *Hunchback* was purchased by the Navy in 1861 and armed with two guns. Because of its shallow draft, the gunboat was continuously used throughout the Civil War. Records of the Office of the Chief Signal Officer (111-B-2011).

Brady Collection. Probably Sergeant Duane Thompson (in the white shirt) of the 23rd New York Infantry and group. 1861. Records of the Office of the Chief Signal Officer (111-B-5423).

George N. Barnard. "Confederate works in front of Atlanta, Georgia." 1864(?). Records of the War Department General and Special Staffs (165-SC-39).

Brady Collection. "Ruins of Georgia RR Roundhouse at Atlanta." 1864. The locomotives are abandoned Confederate units left after the railroad facilities were destroyed just before the Federal capture of the city. Records of the Office of the Chief Signal Officer (111-B-4748).

Selmar Rush Seibert. "Bay Street, Charleston, S.C." 1865. Records of the Office of the Chief of Engineers (77-F-193-2-47).

Brady Collection. "Section of Keystone Battery" or the Keystone Independent Battery Light Artillery. 1862-63. Records of the Office of the Chief Signal Officer (111-B-322).

George N. Barnard. "North Western Depot, Charleston, S.C." 1865. Records of the War Department General and Special Staffs (165-C-780).

Photographer unknown. The *Chickamauga.* 1864. A lightly armed Army transport, it carried supplies along the Tennessee River. Records of the War Department General and Special Staffs (165-C-607).

Photographer unknown. Deck of the screw steamer *Liberty.* May 28, 1864. The boat was chartered frequently by the United States government to ship cargo, mail, and me
Records of the War Department General and Special Staffs (165-C-636).

rady Collection. "Between decks on transport." 1861-65. The men are probably Union soldiers going home on furlough after hospitalization. Records of the Office of the Chief Signal Officer (111-B-5234).

Brady Collection. General Martin T. McMahon, seated in fringed chair, and staff of six. 1865-66. Records of the Office of the Chief Signal Officer (111-B-38).

Brady Collection. House of Representatives managers of the impeachment proceedings and trial of President Andrew Johnson. Taken in Brady's studio on Pennsylvania Avenue in Washington, D.C. 1868. Shown standing, from left to right: James Falconer Wilson, Iowa (1828-1895); George Sewel Boutwell, Mass. (1818-1905); John Alexander Logan, Ill. (1826-1886). Seated, from left to right: Benjamin Franklin Butler, Mass. (1818-1893); Thaddeus Stevens, Pa. (1792-1868); Thomas Williams, Pa. (1806-1872); John Armor Bingham, Ohio (1815-1900). Records of the Office of the Chief Signal Officer (111-B-4279).

Sam A. Cooley. "Store for Freedmen. Beaufort, S.C." Dec. 18, 1864. Records of the War Department General and Special Staffs (165-C-393).

William Henry Jackson. "Photographing in High Places." Tetons Range.
1872. Records of the Geological Survey (57-HS-172).

John K. Hillers. "Grand Cañon, Colorado River, Ariz." 1871-79.
Records of the Geological Survey (57-PS-66).

William Henry Jackson. "A group of all the members of the [Hayden] survey made while camping in Red Buttes." 1870. Fredrick V. Hayden is seated at the far end of the table. William Henry Jackson is standing on the right. Records of the Geological Survey (57-HS-283).

Carleton E. Watkins. Yosemite Valley, Calif. 1866. Records of the National Park Service (79-BC-149).

John K. Hillers. "The Three Brothers, Yosemite Valley." Calif. 1871–79.
Records of the Geological Survey (57-PS-33).

John K. Hillers. "Yosemite National Park, Calif. Cathedral Spires in Yosemite Valley.
1871–79. Records of the Geological Survey (57-PS-28).

Timothy H. O'Sullivan. "Cañon de Chelle. Walls of the Grand Cañon about 1200 feet in height." Lt. George M. Wheeler Expedition of 1873. Records of the Chief of Engineers (77-WA-12).

E. O. Beaman. "The Heart of Lodore, Green River." 1871. Frederick S. Dellenbaugh seated on the bank. Records of the Geological Survey (57-PS-428).

Timothy H. O'Sullivan. Wagon "darkroom" in the Carson Desert, Nev. About 1868. Records of the Office of the Chief of Engineers (77-KS-P-46).

Carleton E. Watkins. The Grizzly Giant, Mariposa Grove, Calif. 1866.
Records of the National Park Service (79-BC-166).

Timothy H. O'Sullivan.
"Ancient Ruins in the Cañon de Chelle, N.M. [New Mexico Territory,
later Arizona]. In a niche 50 feet above present Cañon bed." Lt. George M. Wheele[r]
Expedition of 1873. Records of the Office of the Chief of Engineers (77-WA-11).

J. Lubken. "The native fisherman of the Colorado River, fishing in the Imperial Canal." Aug. 16, 1907. Records of the Bureau of Reclamation (115-JI-323).

Timothy H. O'Sullivan. "Navaho Group." Canyon de Chelly, Ariz. 1873. Records of the Smithsonian Institution (106-WB-305).

35

John K. Hillers. "Terraced Houses at Walpi." Hopi Pueblo, Walpi, Ariz. About 1879. Records of the U.S. Regular Army Mobile Units, 1821–1942 (391-JKH-1).

ohn K. Hillers. "A Moki, weaving." 1879.
Records of the Smithsonian Institution (106-IN-2435b).

Photographer unknown. "Silver Springs Florida, Marion Co." 1871-79.
Records of the Geological Survey (57-PS-115).

A.J. Buck. "Eighteen miles from Stanton. 'Board and lodging' en route for Stanton." Fort Stanton, N.M. Date unknown. Records of the Public Health Service (90-G-94-1

. J. Lubken. "Trappers and hunters in the Four Peak country on Brown's Basin." Salt River Project, Ariz. Jan. 1908. Records of the Bureau of Reclamation (115-JAA-2667).

W. J. Lubken. "Forest service ranger at home." Wallowa National Forest, Ore. About 1908-09. Records of the Forest Service (95-G-81994).

Studio of F. Gutekunst. "Showing scenes at Niagara Falls and in the vicinity." About 1880. Records of the Office of the Chief of Engineers (77-HMS-199F-CN11389).

Photographer unknown. "Oklahoma Ave., Guthrie looking west from Division St." Okla. April 1893. Records of the Office of the Secretary of the Interior (48-RST-7B-31).

W. A. Flower Photograph Gallery. "Opening the Cherokee strip in Oklahoma Territory." Guthrie, Oklahoma Territory. 1893. Records of the Bureau of Land Management (49-AR-26).

W. J. Lubken. "Saloons and disreputable places of Hazen." Newlands Project, Nev. June 6, 1905. Records of the Bureau of Reclamation (115-JQ-389).

OLD MON 26.

Photographer unknown. "Old Mon[ument] 26 Looking E." Mexican–United States border at Nogales, Ariz. About 1893. Records of Boundary and Claims Commissions and Arbitrations (76-MM-19, box 41).

C. C. Jones. "Derailed locomotive as viewed from the east. Damage done by earthquake of August 31, 1886." Ten Mile Hill, Berkeley Co., S.C. Sept. 3–7, 1886. Records of the Geological Survey (57-PS-9).

John K. Hillers. "Santa Fe Railroad Bridge over Canyon Diablo, Arizona, showing train and signs of Albuquerque, New Mexico, clothing stores, etc., painted on Canyon Wall." 1871-78. Records of the Geological Survey (57-PS-109).

C.C. Jones. "Encampment of citizens in city park during earthquake of August 31, 1886, Charleston, Charleston County, South Carolina." Aug. 31, 1886. Records of the Geological Survey (57-PS-27).

Photographer unknown. "Lt. Colonel [William R.] King's Electro Magnet." Willets Point, N.Y. Dec. 6, 1887. Records of the Office of the Chief of Engineers (77-A-12-14).

Photographer unknown. "Century Oil Company." Kern River District, Calif. About 1898. Records of the Bureau of Land Management (49-KRA-2-2).

Charles Waldock. "Newport and Cincinnati Railroad and Wagon Road Bridge." Cincinnati, Ohio. Nov. 27, 1870. Records of the Office of the Chief of Engineers (77-HCS-151F).

Photographer unknown. "Interior of Palace Car—Ohio Railway." About 1875. General Records of the Department of State (59-HB-19).

Photographer unknown. Probably Henry T. Thurber, Private Secretary to President Cleveland, and family. Date unknown. Records of the Public Buildings Service (121-BA-33).

Photographer unknown. "Mr. Carlisle, son of the Secretary of the Treasury."
About 1895. Records of the Public Buildings Service (121-BA-2B).

54

Photographer unknown. Portraits of unidentified Indians from Southeastern
Idaho Reservations. 1897. Records of the Bureau of Indian Affairs. 75-SEI-47

75-SEI-59

75-SEI-64

55

56

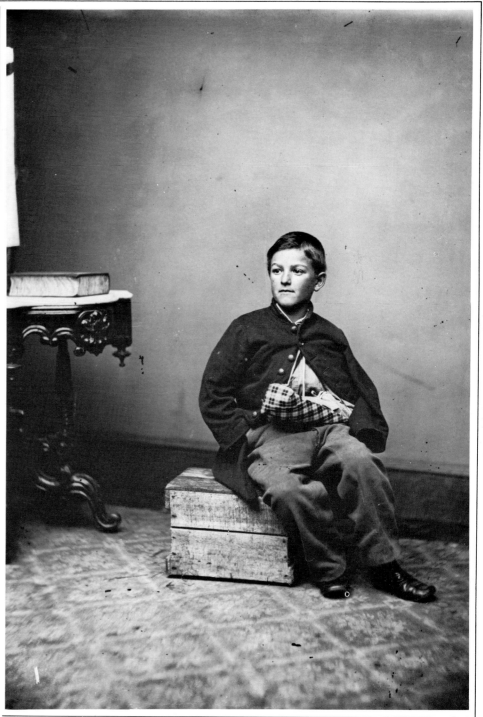

Brady Collection. William Black, wounded in the Civil War. Date unknown. Records of the Office of the Chief Signal Officer (111-B-2368).

Brady Collection. Walt Whitman. About 1866.
Records of the Office of the Chief Signal Officer (111-B-1672).

Brady Collection. General William Tecumseh Sherman,
wearing on his left arm the mourning sash required of
all military men during the six weeks mourning period for Abraham Lincoln. 1865
Records of the Office of the Chief Signal Officer (111-B-1769).

rady Collection. Clara Barton. 1866.
ecords of the Office of the Chief Signal Officer (111-B-1857).

Photographer unknown. Frederick Douglass. 1870-75.
Probably copied from a cabinet card. a type of portrait photograph popular
in the late 19th century. Records of the Public Buildings Service (121-BA-74).

59

Brady Collection. Members of the first Japanese mission to the United States. 1860.
Records of the Office of the Chief Signal Officer (111–B–2325).

Will Soule. "Navajo Silversmith." About 1870.
Records of the Bureau of Indian Affairs. (75–BAE–2421b–6)

Will Soule. "Lone Bear (Tarlow, Kiowa boy) dressed as Osage." About 1870.
Records of the Bureau of Indian Affairs (75-BAE-1409b).

Will Soule. "Asa-to-yet, Comanche Chief." About 1870.
Records of the Bureau of Indian Affairs (75-BAE-1744c).

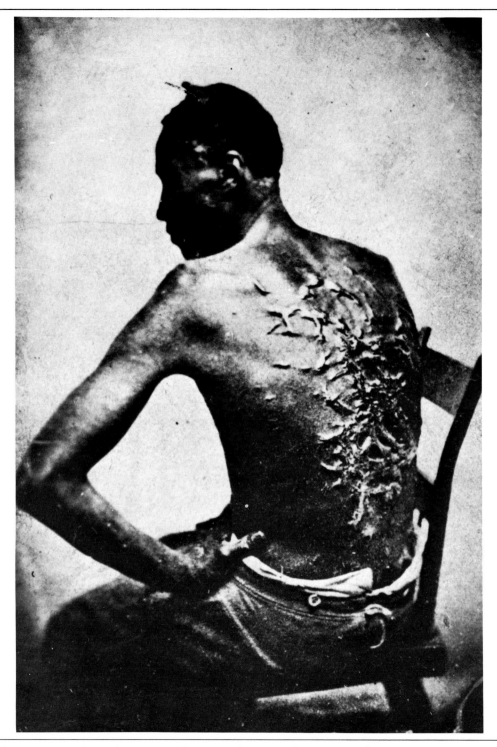

Photographer unknown. The scars from a whipping on a slave's back. 1863. Records of the War Department General and Special Staffs (165-JT-230).

Photographer unknown. "Scene, War Department Exhibit, World's Columbian Exposition, Chicago, Ill." 1893. Records of the Office of the Chief Signal Officer (111-B-3952).

Photographer unknown. "Native Moros, Taluk Samgay, Zamboanga Province, Mindanao." Philippines. 1900. Records of the Office of the Chief Signal Officer (111-RB-1633

.R. Hanna. "Hawaiian Cowboys, Waimea." 1899. From an album prepared to accompany a report on the food products of the Hawaiian Islands. Records of the Office f the Quartermaster General (92-FL-4-4-12).

Photographer unknown. "Drying sardines at Eastport, Me." About 1900. Records of the Fish and Wildlife Service (22-CD-370).

Photographer unknown. "Oyster fleet in Baltimore harbor." About 1900. Records of the Fish and Wildlife Service (22-CE-176).

Photographer unknown. "Crew of New York. Blue fish fishermen." About 1900. Records of the Fish and Wildlife Service (22-CG-269).

Studio of F. Gutekunst. "Scene in a park." Date unknown. Records of the Office of the Chief of Engineers (77-HMS-199-18).

Centennial Photographic Company. From an album, "Photographic Views, U.S. Govt. Building, Army and Navy Exhibit. Centennial Exhibition." Philadelphia. 1876
Records of the War Department General and Special Staffs (165-EP-4).

I. W. Chadwick. "Panorama and views of San Francisco, Cal. Disaster, Earthquake and Fire." 1906. Records of the Office of the Chief Signal Officer (111-AGF-1A-1D).

Photographer unknown. "Third Mississippi River District, Vicksburg, Miss., Fulton Slide." May 1922. Records of the Office of the Chief of Engineers (77-MRC-5-3).

In 1902, the Valdez, Copper River and Yukon Railroad Company contracted with Miles Brothers, a photographic firm of San Francisco and New York, for photograph along a potential railroad line beginning in Valdez, Alaska. The photos are now in the Records of the Office of the Chief Signal Officer.

Miles Brothers. "Native Women and Children on the Kotsina." 1902. (111-AGD-73).

Miles Brothers. "Camp Fire Yarns." 1902 (111-AGD-88).

Miles Brothers. "Public School. Valdez." Oct. 1902 (111-AGD-107).

Miles Brothers. "Some blueberries and a peach." 1902 (111-AGD-104).

S.D. Smith. "Initiating one of the new arrivals at the planting camp." Nebraska Forest. April 1914. Records of the Forest Service (95-G-22227A).

Henry G. Peabody (1856–1951) was a photographer in Pasadena, Calif. In 1905 he incorporated his photographs into a series of slide lectures. After his death, the photograph were donated to the National Park Service, and are now among its records.

Henry G. Peabody. "Reservoir in Canyon Crest Park, Redlands." Calif. About 1900. (79-HPA-253)

Henry G. Peabody. "Bathing at Long Beach." Calif. About 1900. (79-HPA-254)

Henry G. Peabody. "Sutro Baths, San Francisco." Calif. About 1900. (79-HPA-106)

. J. Lubken. "Racing at Yakima Fair." Yakima Project, Wash. Sept. 27, 1907. Records of the Bureau of Reclamation (115-JAI-428).

W. J. Lubken. "Boating on Lake Roosevelt, or Tonto reservoir, just above Roosevelt dam." Salt River Project, Ariz. April 1909. Records of the Bureau of Reclamatio
(115-JAA-1847).

Paul J. Fair. "Sunday Morning in Lake Basin Public Camp." Cleveland National Forest, Calif. 1922. Records of the Forest Service (95-G-164475).

Harry E. Hill. "Short-nosed sturgeon, caught in Indian River, near Fort Pierce, Florida." 1902. Records of the Fish and Wildlife Service (22-MSF-8).

H. T. Cory. "The home of Project Manager, L. H. Mitchell." On the Lower Yellowstone Project in Montana and North Dakota. Sept. 18, 1914. Records of the Bureau of Reclamation (115-JM-631).

R.C. Huey. "Typical mountaineer family of the industrious farming class and occupying the most productive lands." Ark. June 1914. Records of the Forest Service 95-G-18909A).

H. T. Cory. "Harvesting wheat on McClellan Ranch." Carlsbad Project, N.M. June 16, 1916. Records of the Bureau of Reclamation (115–JD–315).

hotographer unknown. The waterfront at St. Louis, taken on an inspection trip of the Mississippi River Commission. Oct. 25, 1909. Records of the Office of the Chief of ngineers (77-H-l0580P-1).

W. J. Lubken. "Government automobile, in front of Adams Hotel, Phoenix." Salt River Project, Ariz. March 23, 1907. Records of the Bureau of Reclamation (115-JAA-1115

hotographer unknown. "Poultry Inspection." About 1910. Records of the Food and Drug Administration (88-GN-C156).

Sy Seidman. "Ellis Island. N.Y. Line inspection of arriving aliens." 1923. Records of the Public Health Service (90-G-885).

Photographer unknown. "Banana Inspection." About 1910. Records of the Food and Drug Administration (88-GC-1608).

Photographer unknown. "Darkies with brooms of bambusa, on Latimer's place, Belton, S.C." Sept. 29, 1899. Records of the Bureau of Agricultural Economics (83-FB-272

photographer unknown. "Meridian Hill Park. View showing texture of concrete in lower wall. Maid with small children in view." Washington, D.C. About 1910. Records of he Office of Public Buildings and Public Parks of the National Capital (42-SPB-18).

Photographer unknown. Secretary of the Treasury Lyman Gage. Saturday, July 2, 1898. Records of the Public Buildings Service (121-BA-97K).

Photographer unknown. Trimming currency. 1907. Records of the Public Buildings Service (121-BA-361B).

Minneapolis General Electric Co.
Meter Readers.
August 31–'18

Photographer unknown. Counting money inside a vault in the Treasury Department. About 1907. Records of the Public Buildings Service (121-BA-358B).

Photographer unknown. "Four women standing to exhibit meter reader uniforms Minneapolis General Electric Company. Aug. 31, 1918. Records of the Women's Bureau (86-G-11D-1).

ewis Hine. "Addie Laird, 12 years old. Spinner in a Cotton Mill. Girls in mill say
e is 10 years old..." North Pownal, Vt. Feb. 9, 1910. Records of the Children's
ureau (102-LH-1056).

F. P. Burke. "Negro women weighing wire coils and recording weights, to establish
wage rates." April 16, 1919. Records of the Women's Bureau (86-G-5L-1).

Lewis Hine. "Breaker boys working in Ewen Breaker." Mine in S. Pittston, Pa. Jan. 10, 1911. Records of the Children's Bureau (102-LH-1941).

hotographer unknown. "Class 'E9' Ingersoll drill at work in diversion channel." Minidoka Project, Idaho and Wyo. July 30, 1905. Records of the Bureau of Reclamation 15-JO-187).

W. J. Lubken. "Raising and lowering gates at newly completed diversion dam at head of main Truckee canal on Truckee river at the opening of the Truckee-Carson project Newlands Project, Western Nev. June 17, 1905. Records of the Bureau of Reclamation (115-JQ-178).

Attributed to Ernest Hallen. "Looking north, from gate, upper east chamber." Jan. 14, 1913. Miraflores, construction of the Panama Canal. Records of the Panama Canal (185-G-2003).

Photographer unknown. "Claude Grahame-White, October 14, 1910, starting on return trip to Benning after visiting the Executive Offices." Records of the Office of the Chief Signal Officer (11-RB-5118).

Dewell Photo Company. "Mechanics, Air Mail Service, Omaha, Neb." 1924. Records of the Post Office Department (28-MS-2B-8).

Swenson Studio. "First sack. Lindbergh and Green loading cargo." 1925. The inaugural flight of contract air mail from St. Louis to Chicago. Lambert Field, St. Louis, M[...]
Records of the Post Office Department (28-MS-3A-11).

Photographer unknown. "Saying Good Bye to Sweetheart." 1917. Records of the War Department General and Special Staffs (165-WW-476-21).

Photographer unknown. "Colored women open a club to care for their men in the service." Newark, N.J. About 1918. Records of the War Department General ar
Special Staffs (165-WW-127-49).

Photographer unknown. "Gun Crew from Regimental Headquarters Company, 23rd Infantry, firing 37mm gun during an advance against German entrenched positions." 1918. Records of the Office of the Chief Signal Officer (111-SC-94980).

Photographer unknown. "The American Advance in the Argonne. This shattered church in the ruins of Neuvilly, close to the Forest of Argonne, furnished temporary shelter for American wounded, while the struggle that rid the woods of Germans was being waged." 1918. Records of the Office of the Chief Signal Officer (111-SC-24942).

.G. Morper. "Interior of Building where troops of 305th M.P. Train, Co. A, are billeted." Beauval, France. July 1918. Records of the Office of the Chief Signal Officer (11-SC-17409).

R. Gallivan. "Mrs. W. E. Corey playing cards with the wounded officers on the porch. Corey home for Convalescent Officers, Chateau de Villegenis at Palaiseau, France[
Sept. 18, 1918. Mrs. Corey, or Mabelle Gilman, an actress, was the wife of the president of Carnegie Steel Company and United States Steel. Records of the Office of the Chi[
Signal Officer (111-SC-23400).

Photographer unknown. "Women's Activities in Arsenals, Etc. Acetylene Welding on Cylinder Water Jacket." 1918. Records of the Office of the Chief Signal Officer (111-SC-35757).

Photographer unknown. "164th Depot Brigade, Camp Funston, Kansas." 1918-19. Records of the War Department General and Special Staffs (165-WW-78G-2).

Paul Thompson. "Douglas Fairbanks, the well known motion picture actor speaking on the third Liberty Loan at the Sub-Treasury Bldg. New York." April 1918. Records of the War Department General and Special Staffs (165-WW-240F-1).

The Schreiber Company. "Traffic Policeman using 4th Lib[erty] Loan fans for signals." Oct. 1918. Records of the Bureau of the Public Debt (53-LL-3).

Photographer unknown. "Elsie Ferguson in 'The Spirit That Wins.'" 1917–18. Records of the Bureau of the Public Debt (53-LL-4).

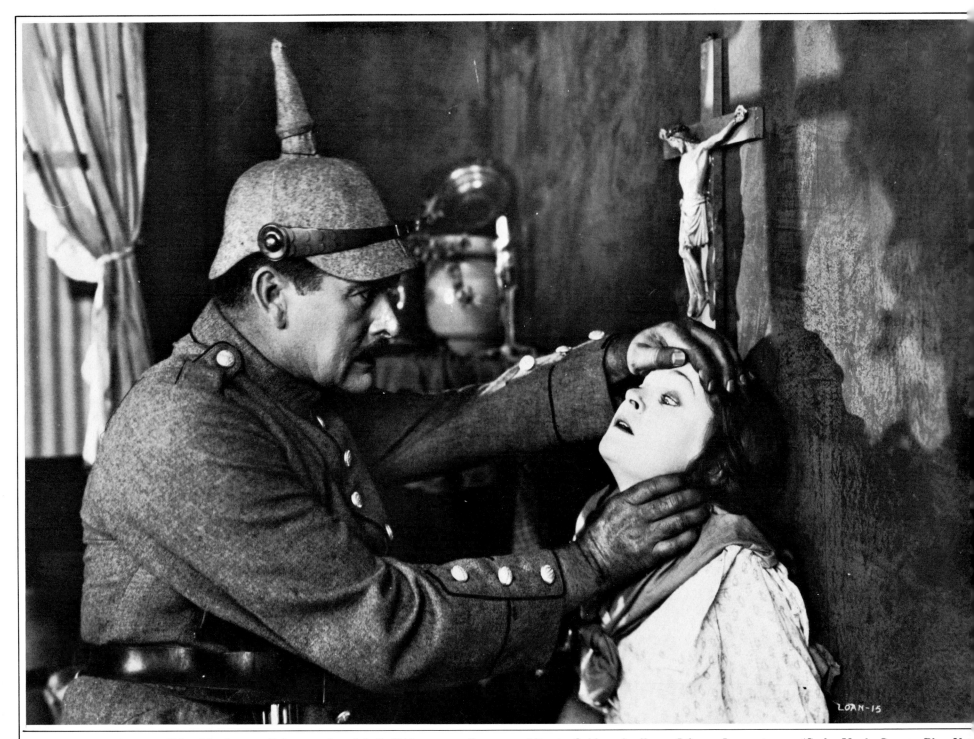

Photographer unknown. "Mae Marsh, as a Belgian girl and A.C. Gibbons as a German soldier in Goldwyn's all-star Liberty Loan picture, 'Stake Uncle Sam to Play You Hand.'" 1917-18. Records of the Bureau of the Public Debt (53-LL-1).

Photographer unknown. "Percheron, mares." Date unknown. Records of the Office of the Secretary of Agriculture (16-G-65-1-6).

McManigal. "Farm hands at dining table." 1939. Records of the Office of the Secretary of Agriculture (16-G-163-1-2).

Photographer unknown. "Picking cotton." Tallulah, La. 1924–25. Records of the Office of the Secretary of Agriculture (16-G-116-1-CI19092).

George W. Ackerman. "Community cotton gin owned and operated by Negroes, Madison County, Alabama." 1923. Records of the Office of the Secretary of Agricultur (16-G-115-2-S2567C).

George W. Ackerman. "Cultivating cotton demonstration, Richland County, South Carolina." May 17, 1932. Records of the Federal Extension Service (33–FRA–S15895C).

Photographer unknown. "Wheat field dressed with nitrate of soda." 1936. Records of the Bureau of Foreign and Domestic Commerce and Successor Agencies (151-FC-96A-

George W. Ackerman. "Picking peanuts from the vines, Terrell Co., Ga." Nov. 13, 1929. Records of the Federal Extension Service (33-SC-13306).

Sloan. "Buried machinery in barn lot." Dallas, S.D. May 13, 1936. Records of the Soil Conservation Service (114-SD-5089).

Harmon. "'Okies' car driving through town." Amarillo, Tex. July 1941. Records of the Agricultural Stabilization and Conservation Service (145-AAA-7434).

Photographer unknown. "Texas cotton picking family looking for cotton to pick." Sept. 1931. Records of the Federal Extension Service (33-SC-15691).

Photographer unknown. "These loggers for Hammond Lumber Company are proud of the climbing ability of their 'Caterpillar' logging cruiser and posed thus for the cameraman." Oct. 1928. Records of the Bureau of Foreign and Domestic Commerce and Successor Agencies (151-FC-98-C1).

Photographer unknown. "Newsboy is shown selling Father Coughlin's own newspaper, 'Social Justice' in front of the 'Shrine of the Little Flower' Catholic Church." Detroit, Mich. July 1940. Records of the Work Projects Administration (69-GU-279).

Dorothea Lange. "Newly-built store and trading center typical of new shacktown community." Riverbank, San Joaquin Valley, Calif. April 9, 1940. Records of the Bureau of Agricultural Economics (83-G-41450).

Irving Rusinow. "Community studies. Interiors and interior activities." Harmony Community, Putnam Co., Ga. May 28–June 1, 1941. Records of the Bureau of Agricultur Economics (83-G-41094).

ving Rusinow. "Community studies. Interior and interior activities." Harmony
ommunity, Putnam Co., Ga. May 28–June 1, 1941. Records of the Bureau of
gricultural Economics (83-G-41089).

George W. Ackerman. "Farm woman using a small modern churn." Stephens Co.,
Okla. July 1935. Records of the Federal Extension Service (33-SC-19679).

Irving Rusinow. "One room school at Versylvania is a converted two room dwelling. Of 15 pupils, six were absent the day picture was taken." Taos Co., N.M. Dec. 194
Records of the Bureau of Agricultural Economics (83-G-41768).

Photographer unknown. "Boy, Broom and Butterbeans." 1939.
Records of the Work Projects Administration (69-GU-976).

J.G. Curtis. "Pittsburgh, Pa. Unsightly advertising (before)." Date unknown.
Records of the Forest Service (95-G-95580).

Dorothea Lange. "Roadside settlement in commercial pea district on Highway #33." San Joaquin Valley, Calif. April 9, 1940. Records of the Bureau of Agricultural Econom (83-G-41563).

Dorothea Lange. "Children in a democracy. A migratory family living in a trailer in an open field. No sanitation, no water. They came from Amarillo, Texas." Nov. 1940. Records of the Bureau of Agricultural Economics (83-G-44360).

P. Sekaer. "Rural Electrification Cooperative Office." Lafayette, La. 1939. Records of the Office of the Secretary of Agriculture (16-G-112-2-S3522A).

otographer unknown. "Sometimes the whole family gathered around the receiving set. This Hood River County, Oregon, farm family is listening to the radio." July 20, 25. Records of the Federal Extension Service (33-SC-4849).

Photographer unknown. "Walnuts—types of, variety." Date unknown. Records of the Bureau of Plant Industry, Soils, and Agricultural Engineering (54-G-2632A).

Photographer unknown. "Annual Muscadine Grape Exhibit. U.S. Dept. of Agriculture. Wash. D.C." Jan. 1919. Records of the Bureau of Plant Industry, Soils, and Agricultural Engineering (54–G–19168).

Daniel J. Sheehan. "Herbert Hoover flyfishing for steelhead trout." Klamath River, Calif. 1933. Records of the Forest Service (95-G-285193).

Lewis W. Hine. "Building Rubber Doll Molds." Dec. 1936–July 1937. Records of the Work Projects Administration (69-RP-57).

Lewis W. Hine. "Singer Power Machine Sewing Group." Dec. 1936–July 1937. Records of the Work Projects Administration (69-RP-56).

ouis R. Bostwick. "View of row of operators. View of chairs showing type of chairs used by telephone co." April 7, 1927. Records of the Women's Bureau (86-G-10-F-15).

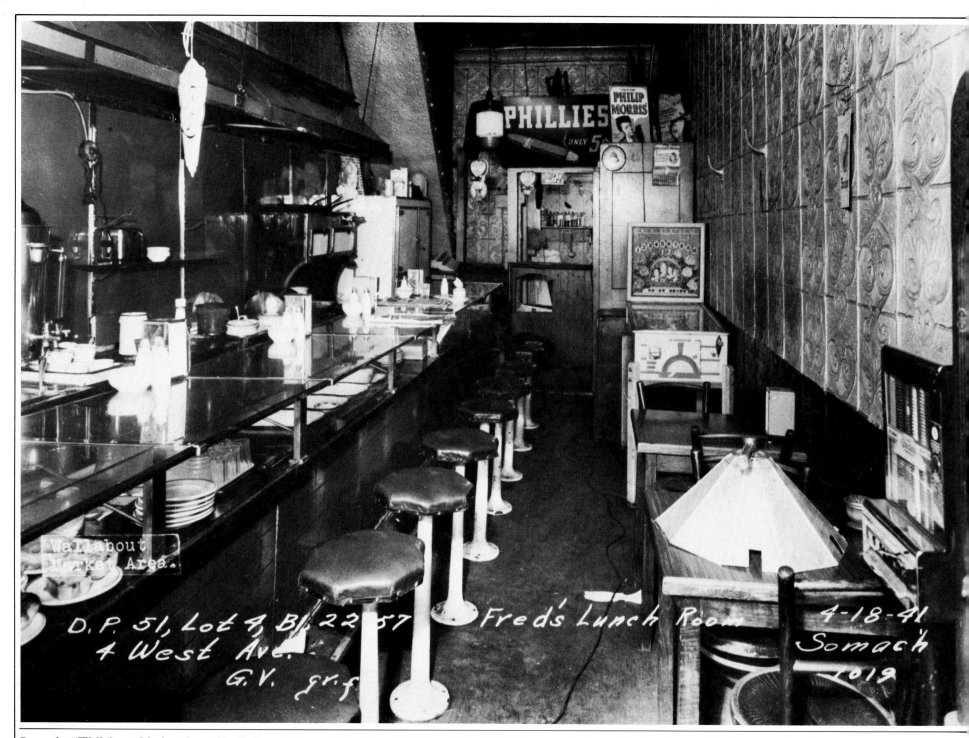

Somach. "Wallabout Market Area. Fred's Lunch Room." Brooklyn, N.Y. April 18, 1941. Photographed prior to demolition to make room for the expansion of the New York Navy Yard. Records of Naval Districts and Shore Establishments (181-WM-1A-1019).

David Robbins. "Along the Waterfront." New York, N.Y. Jan. 3, 1937. Records of the Work Projects Administration (69–ANP–13–P759–70).

Photographer unknown. "New York City Crime Prevention Photos of Juvenile Aid Bureau—South Harlem Unit—Water shot—street activities." Aug. 8, 1937. Records of the Work Projects Administration (69-N-16195-D).

Photographer unknown. "New York City, Crime Prevention Photos of Juvenile Aid Bureau—Delinquents gambling. From Police Department of New York City." May 18, 1937. Records of the Work Projects Administration (69-N-16171-D).

Photographer unknown. "Cities and towns at night." New York. Date unknown. Records of the Agricultural Stabilization and Conservation Service (145-AAA-7779W).

Photographer unknown. Installation of the statue of Abraham Lincoln in the Lincoln Memorial, Washington, D.C. 1920. Records of the Office of Public Buildings and Public Parks of the National Capital (42-M-J-1).

Photographer unknown. "Formation—Keystone Bombardment Airplanes of 2nd Bombardment Group over Washington, D.C." April 23, 1931. Records of the Army Air Forces (18-AN-15994).

Photographer unknown. "Big Tujunga Wash, North Curve Riverside Drive at Bellflower Avenue." May 1938. From a series of airscapes of flooding in California. Records of the Army Air Forces (18-AA-191-45).

hotographer unknown. "USS *Akron* in flight over New York City, N.Y." About 1932. General Records of the Department of the Navy, 1798–1947 (80-G-458713).

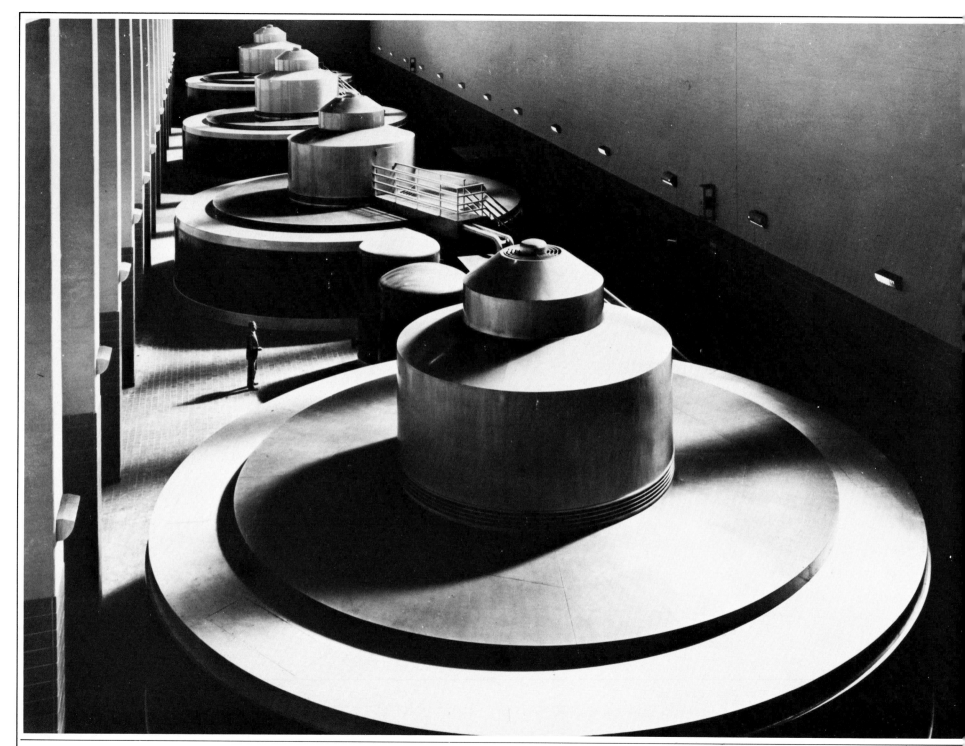

Photographer unknown. Pickwick Dam, Tenn. Date unknown. Records of the Tennessee Valley Authority (142-RS-25-2).

nsel Adams. Grand Canyon National Park, Ariz. 1941. Records of the National Park Service (79-AAF-3).

Photographer unknown. From a collection of Panoramic Views of Indian Schools, Bureau of Personnel, and U.S. Public Health Service Facilities. 1904–31. Records of t Bureau of Indian Affairs (75-PA-10-1).

Photographer unknown. "Indians who attended meeting with Mr. Scattergood [Assistant Commissioner of Indian Affairs] and Supt. Arnold [Superintendent of Klama Indian Reservation] at Beatty, Oregon." June 17, 1930. Records of the Bureau of Indian Affairs (75-PA-10-2).

E. D. Goldbeck. 16th U.S. Infantry, Ft. Jay, N.Y. Sept. 28, 1936. Records of the War Department General and Special Staffs (165-PX-1-4274R).

Ansel Adams. Glacier National Park, Mont. 1941. Records of the National Park Service (79-AAF-13).

Russell Lee. "Miners checking in at the lamphouse at completion of morning shift." Kopperston, Wyoming Co., W. V. Aug. 22, 1946. Records of the Solid Fuels Administration for War (245-MS-1765 L).

Coal Mines Administration Survey

In 1946, the Coal Mines Administration conducted a survey of medical, housing, and sanitary conditions in coal mining areas. Noted photographer Russell Lee (1903-   ) was one of several photographers commissioned to document visually the findings of the agency.

Russell Lee. "Milong Bond taking a bath." Harmco, Wyoming Co., W.V. Aug. 23, 1946. Records of the Solid Fuels Administration for War (245-MS-1847 L).

Russell Lee. "In front of the post office waiting for the mail." Bokoshe, Le Flore Co., Okla. July 24, 1946. Records of the Solid Fuels Administration for War (245-MS-1042)

Russell Lee. "Gonzalla Sullivan, miner, with his little boy." Grant Town, Marion Co., V. June 13, 1946. Records of the Solid Fuels Administration for War (245–MS–113L).

Russell Lee. "Son of Clabe Hicks, miner." Bradshaw, McDowell Co., W.V. Aug. 27, 1946. Records of the Solid Fuels Administration for War (245–MS–2010 L).

Russell Lee. "Saturday afternoon street scene." Welch, McDowell Co., W.V. Aug. 24, 1946. Records of the Solid Fuels Administration for War (245-MS-1942 L).

ssell Lee. "Handling serpents at the Pentecostal Church of God." Lejunior, Harlan Co., Ky. Sept. 15, 1946. Records of the Solid Fuels Administration for War (245-MS-2621 L).

Russell Lee. The Blaine Sergent family. Lejunior, Harlan Co., Ky. Sept. 15, 1946. Records of the Solid Fuels Administration for War (245-MS-2802 L).

D. No-Work To-Morrow

ssell Lee. "Blaine Sergent, coal leader, putting up his check at end of day's work." Lejunior, Harlan Co., Ky. Sept. 13, 1946. Records of the Solid Fuels Administration for
r (245-MS-2506 L).

Photographer unknown. "Stars over Berlin and Tokyo will soon replace these factory lights reflected in the noses of America's fighting planes at Douglas Aircraft's Lo Beach, Cal., plant..." About 1943. Records of the Office of War Information (208-AA-352QQ-5).

Photographer unknown. "USS *Shaw* (DD-373) exploding during the Japanese raid on Pearl Harbor." Dec. 7, 1941. General Records of the Department of the Navy, 1798–1947 (30-G-16871).

Rose. "The Invaders Hit the Beach." American troops storm a North African beach. About 1943. Records of the United States Coast Guard (26-G-2326).

Photographer unknown. "Lunchtime at the Vega aircraft plant, Burbank, Calif." Au 1943. General Records of the Department of the Navy, 1798-1947 (80-G-412639).

mitri Kessel(?). "Giant Gears in a shop in Mass[achusetts] will become parts of U.S. warships." About 1943. Records of the Office of War Information (208-PP-15M-1).

Photographer unknown. Huge miniatures of Japanese targets, such as this model of Tokyo Bay in the background, were constructed on sound stages and used in a series special motion pictures produced by the Army Air Forces' Motion Picture Unit to brief crews bombing Tokyo, Nagasaki, Hiroshima, Yokohama and Yokosuka. About 194 Records of the Office of War Information (208-AA-110N-1).

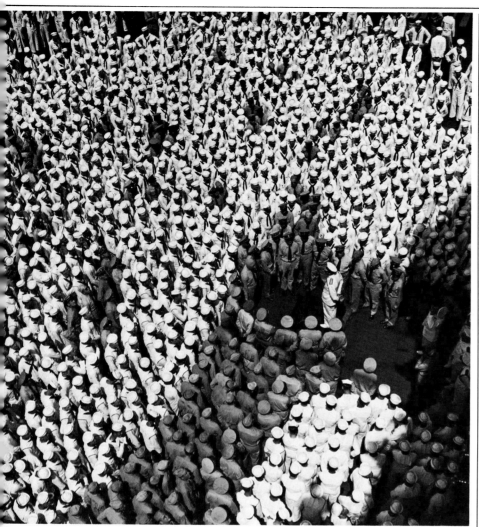

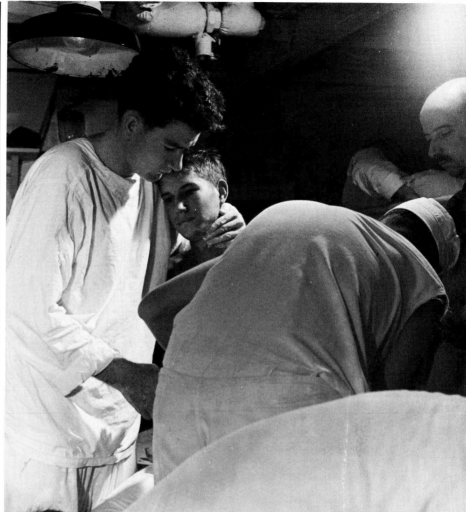

Wayne Miller. "Adm. Lord Louis Mountbatten, R.N., addresses personnel aboard the USS *Saratoga* (CV-3) at Trincomalee, Ceylon." April 29, 1944. General Records of the Department of the Navy, 1798–1947 (80-G-470720).

Photographer unknown. "Pvt. J.B. Slagle, USA, receives his daily dressing of wounds on board USS *Solace* (AH-5) enroute from Okinawa to Guam." April 1945. General Records of the Department of the Navy, 1798–1947 (80-G-413963).

Photographer unknown. "Tank lighters under fire." Saipan. About 1943. Records of the United States Coast Guard (26-G-2502).

Photographer unknown. "U.S.S. *Santa Fe* (CL-60) lays alongside of U.S.S. *Franklin* rendering assistance after carrier had been hit and set afire by a Japanese dive bomber." March 1945. General Records of the Department of the Navy, 1798-1947 (80-G-273880).

Charles Jacobs. "Japanese prisoners of war are bathed, clipped, 'deloused,' and issued GI clothing as soon as they are taken aboard the U.S.S. *New Jersey.*" Dec. 1944. General Records of the Department of the Navy, 1798-1947 (80-G-469956).

Barrett Gallagher. "Burial at sea for the officers and men of the USS *Intrepid* (CV-11) who lost their lives when the carrier was hit by Japanese bombs during operations in the Philippines." Nov. 26, 1944. General Records of the Department of the Navy, 1798-1947 (80-G-468912).

Photographer unknown. "U.S. Marines pinned down on Peliliu." Sept. 22, 1944. General Records of the Department of the Navy, 1798-1947 (80-G-435697).

Photographer unknown. "Hello, Gorgeous! Kimona See Me Sometime." About 1943. Records of the United States Coast Guard (26-G-2477).

lem Albers. "A young evacuee of Japanese ancestry waits with the family baggage before leaving by bus for an assembly center in the spring of 1942." Calif. April 1942.
ecords of the War Relocation Authority (210-G2–A6).

Dorothea Lange. "Members of the Mochida family awaiting evacuation bus." Hayward, Calif. May 8, 1942. Records of the War Relocation Authority (210-G2-C153).

Dorothea Lange. "Dust storm at this War Relocation Authority center [Manzanar] where evacuees of Japanese ancestry are spending the duration." Calif. July 3, 1942.
Records of the War Relocation Authority (210-G10-C839).

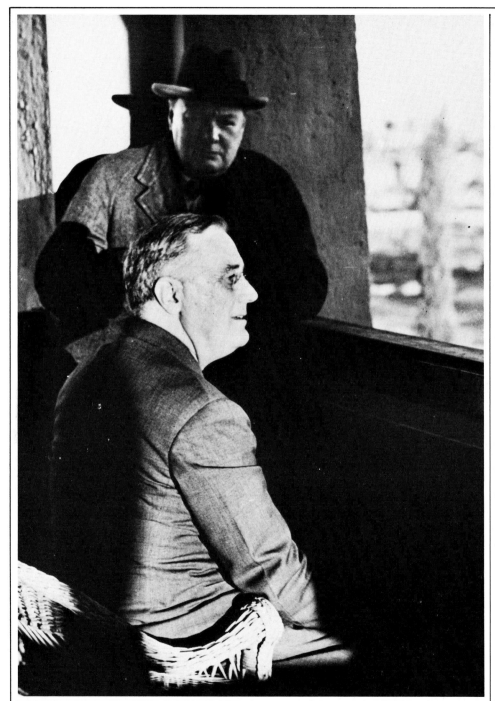

Photographer unknown. "President Roosevelt and Prime Minister Churchill at Marrakech, French Morocco, on Jan. 24, following the Casablanca conference." 1943. General Records of the Department of the Navy, 1798–1947 (80-G-35190).

Photographer unknown. "Navy pilots in the forward elevator well playing basketball." USS *Monterey* (CVL-26) operating in the central Pacific. June–July 1944. General Records of the Department of the Navy, 1798–1947 (80-G-417628).

hotographer unknown. "Uncontrollable exuberance displayed by men of Service Squadron 10 anchored in the western Pacific as news of Japan's willingness to surrender
read through the fleet." Aug. 10, 1945. General Records of the Department of the Navy, 1798-1947 (80-G-700927).

Osborne. "A shack for negroes only at Belle Glade, Fla." April 1945. Records of the Office of the Secretary of Agriculture (16-N-6435).

Photographer unknown. "Atomic cloud during Baker Day blast at Bikini." July 25, 1946. General Records of the Department of the Navy, 1798–1947 (80-G-396229).

Photographer unknown. "Beach crowds as seen from the Parachute Jump at Steeplechase Park." Coney Island, N.Y. 1950. Records of the United States Information Agenc(306-PS-50-7260).

otographer unknown. "New York City. Showing the construction of the Esso Building as iron workers raise steel at 32nd floor." 1954. Records of the United States Infor-
tion Agency (306-PS-54-186).

Photographer unknown. "Truck refueling at night at eastbound Esso Midway station. Pennsylvania Turnpike, Bedford, Penn." May 1945. Records of the Bureau of Public Roads (30-N-47-90-C).

Photographer unknown. "Night scene." Date unknown. Records of the Rural Electrification Administration (221-REA-13761).

Russell Lee. "Children of miners." Huerfano Co., Colo. June 29, 1946. Records of the Solid Fuels Administration for War (245-MS-405 L).

Photographer unknown. "Patriotic residents on the west side pose in front of their homes under a long line of American flags on the Fourth of July, 1961. There are 36 houses the block and 38 flags were flown." Chicago, Ill. 1961. United Press International. From the Records of the United States Information Agency (306-PS-62-584).

Photographer unknown. "Independence, Mo. Night view of downtown Independence looking west showing Lexington Avenue on the south side of Courthouse Square." 195
Records of the United States Information Agency (306-PS-51-8369).

bie Rowe. President Eisenhower with Helen Keller and Polly Thompson. Nov. 3, 1953. Records of the National Park Service (79-AR-2196-A).

Don Phelan. The photographer and his family watch a debate between John F. Kennedy and Richard Nixon during the presidential campaign. Sept. 26, 1960. Unit Press International. Records of the United States Information Agency (306-PS-60-16872).

Abbie Rowe. The funeral of President John F. Kennedy. Mrs. Kennedy and children leaving the White House. Nov. 25, 1963. Records of the National Park Service (79-AR-8255-1B).

Photographer unknown. March on Washington for Jobs and Freedom. Aug. 28, 1963. Records of the United States Information Agency (306-SS-28B-35-6).

Photographer unknown. Crowd at the Washington Monument during the March on Washington for Jobs and Freedom. Aug. 28, 1963. Records of the United States Information Agency (306-SS-28B-45-30).

INDEX TO PHOTOGRAPHERS

ORDERING INFORMATION

Most of these photographs are in the public domain. Reproductions may, therefore, be ordered at a nominal cost. When this book went to press, an 8″ x 10″ print was available for under $5.00. Current prices, and further information, may be obtained by writing to the Still Picture Branch (NNVP), National Archives, Washington, D.C. 20408. Please include the file number, given at the end of each caption, in any inquiries about specific photographs.

The National Archives would like to thank the National Association of Photographic Manufacturers, Inc., for its generous financial and technical support for the exhibition on which this book is based. The following companies, through the National Association, helped make the exhibit possible:

American Can Company
Bell & Howell Company
Berkey Photo, Inc.
CX Systems
Da-Lite Screen Company, Inc.
E. I. du Pont de Nemours & Co., Inc.
Eastman Kodak Company
GAF Corporation
General Electric Company
GTE Sylvania Incorporated
Helion Industries, Inc.
Hudson Photographic Industries Inc.
Ilford Inc.
Imperial Camera Corp.
ITT Photo Products
Keuffel & Esser Company
Keystone Camera Corporation
La Belle Industries, Inc.

Macbeth Division
Mallory Battery Company
Metacomet, Incorporated
3M Company
Nashua Corporation
North American Phillips Lighting Corporation
Pako Corporation
Peerless Photo Products, Inc.
Picker Chemicals Inc.
Polaroid Corporation
Polychrome Corporation
Powers Chemco, Inc.
Rolev Corporation
Smith-Victor Corporation
Tiffen Manufacturing Corporation
Union Carbide Corporation
Westinghouse Electric Corporation